AF663417

Behind Psychology

Searching for the Roots

Attention Authors

Manas Publications is fighting a war to tell the world that India can win the battle not only by bullet but also by pen. We are converting fighters into writers since our country is full of intellectuals but their knowledge is only confined to them. No sincere effort has been made by any publisher to give the right direction to their knowledge and the talent of intellectual is still hidden. An author always gives the raw material in the shape of manuscript and it is the sense of publisher to make it a finished product. We are motivating the intellectuals' mind and publishing their manuscripts for more than two decades and would like to publish your manuscript too. If you or your colleagues have any manuscript or are working on, please don't hesitate to contact us with detailed synopsis and contents for its publication. We take utmost care in production and give a wide publicity to the book and its author. We can also suggest you the title for writing related to your subject, since we are the publishers who believe more in quality than in quantity.

Behind Psychology

Searching for the Roots

Vijay Singal, IRS
Commissioner of Income Tax
Delhi

Manas Publications
New Delhi-110 002 (INDIA)

MANAS PUBLICATIONS
(We Convert Fighters into Writers)
(Publishers for IAS, IPS, IFS, IRS, Defence, Press, Judges etc)

4402/5-A, Ansari Road (Opp HDFC Bank)
Darya Ganj, New Delhi-110 002 (India)
Off.: 23260783, 23265523, Fax: 011-23272766
E-mail: manaspublications@gmail.com
manaspublications@yahoo.com

© VK Singal, IRS

2013 (FP-2002)

ISBN: 81-7049-145-2

Rs. 295/-

No part of this book can be reproduced, stored in a retrieval system or transmitted in any form, by any means, including mechanical/printing, electronic, photocopying, recording, or otherwise, without the prior written permission of the Publisher.

The views expressed in this book are those of the Contributors/ Author(s) and not at all of the publisher. The publisher is not responsible for the views of the Author and authenticity of the data, in any way whatsoever.

Cataloguing/listing of this book for re-sale purpose can be done, only by the authorised companies

All disputes are subject to Delhi jurisdiction only.

Designed at
Manas Publications

Printed in India at
RK Offset, Delhi and published by
Mrs Suman Lata for Manas Publications,
4402/5-A, Ansari Road (Opp HDFC Bank),
Darya Ganj, New Delhi-110 002 (INDIA)

Dedicated to Shanti, My Mother

Acknowledgements

The writing of this book would not have become possible without the help and blessings of well-wishers. I started working on this project only when Nitish convinced me that I am capable of doing it. Honourable Justice Shri S.Ranganathan, Mrs. Saroj Bala, Shri S.K. Mishra, Shri A. K. Garg, Shri O. P. Garg, Shri Sanjeeva Narayan, Shri J. K. Bansal, Miss Ruhi Garg and Shri Mahesh Shairwal have gone through the manuscript at different stages of completion and their suggestions have proved very useful in improving the quality of this work.

Shri R. K. Tayal has devoted lots of his time and energy for the completion of this book. His untiring efforts have been of great help.

Shri D.K.Das was nice enough to spare his time for preparation of the sketches. Shri Ajay Sood was instrumental in getting these drawings prepared.

Anju, Nishant and Suhail have contributed their labour in typing and re-typing. Special thanks are due to my wife, Nautasha Singal, for her overall support.

Seek solutions, not salvation

Dr. Karan Singh
MEMBER OF PARLIAMENT
(RAJYA SABHA)

3, NYAYA MARG
CHANAKYAPURI
NEW DELHI - 110 021

FOREWORD

What is the purpose of life and what is an individual's role in it? Who created all this and what is an individual's relationship with Him? These and other such questions arose thousands of years ago in the Himalayas and classical Greece, specially in the minds of sensitive and sincere people down to the present day. Such questions are uncomfortable as neither is it easy to find convincing answers nor is it possible to ignore them. Generations of scientists, philosophers, religious and spiritual leaders have spent their lives in trying to solve some of these riddles, but curiously they have often reached different, sometimes even contradictory conclusions.

Shri Vijay Singal has made an effort through his work ***Searching for the Roots*** to examine some of these issues in a logical fashion, and this study has led to the emergence of some revealing hypotheses. While no one can bring any finality to such questions and their suggested answers, it is hoped that this small book will contribute its mite towards the eternal discussion about the concept of life and the deeper significance of the human experience.

Karan Singh

Be, not only, proud of your own existence
But be, also, the pride of Existence

Introduction

One of the aims of all sciences, in fact of all knowledge, is to suggest answers to questions which often arise in the human mind. But what is generally not realised is that, most of the times, the answers are hidden in the questions themselves. The questions, when raised in a systematic manner, tend to find their own answers. Under the guidance of aware reasoning, seemingly intricate problems of life become capable of searching their own solutions. Not only that. Through an aware understanding of the creation, one can as well come face to face with the Creator Himself.

Based on this belief, an effort has been made, through this book, to try to understand the intricacies of the complex network of existence – the creation.

For the sake of convenience of the reader, this book has been divided into eight chapters. First two chapters have tried to explore the origin of life. How all-pervading consciousness starts manifesting itself and how, through various permutations and combinations of different forms of matter and energy, life comes into being. At some stage of evolutionary process, there comes into being an organic entity which is not only aware of it's own existence, but also of other organic and inorganic creatures. Being aware, it creates an image of itself, which puts it apart from the rest of the universe. That is how an ego is born.

Since the medium through which an ego can arise and survive is awareness, only an aware being can have an ego. The ego which defines one's personality is a highly dynamic concept, since it depends mainly on three factors, which themselves are always in a flux. These factors are one's environment, experience and will power.

The third chapter examines the nature, and makes a comparative study of self and ego, and also of conscious and subconscious mind. It also discusses as to how knowledge of these subjects, and enhanced awareness about them, can help one to manage oneself well, and thereby to lead a personally satisfying and socially beneficial life.

Chapters four and five deal with the subject of relationship of the individual with the Creator. Everyone, including the Creator Himself, is governed by the same laws, that is, laws of nature. These laws are universally applicable, and exception, if any, is only an illusion.

Chapter six explains how everyone is caught in a vicious circle of illogical thought and action and how, through enhanced awareness, one can not only break this circle, but also enter a virtuous spheroid where one attains a perfectly peaceful state of mind.

Chapter seven examines the web of relationships in which an individual is seemingly entrapped. Relationship is a multi-dimensional and dynamic concept. Of all the creatures, only human beings are capable of entering into relationships with abstract entities.

In the last chapter, an effort has been made to answer some frequently raised questions.

No treatise on philosophy or for that matter on any social science can claim to provide definite answers to questions it raises. But, it surely can set the ball of inquiry rolling. It would be a matter of great satisfaction if this work succeeds in this object.

Life is a gift of Nature,
Your appreciation can be a good return

CONTENTS

Notes

The source of your strengths is yourself;
Discover it.
The source of your weaknesses is the thought of weakness;
Overcome it.

H
O
H2O
Dipak Das

One

Origin of Ego

How The Creation Came Into Being

Entire Creation is the result of a continuous interaction between two basic elements of existence, namely matter and energy, in the same manner as zeros and ones of the binary system constitute the virtual world of the Internet. Just as various permutations and combinations of zeros and ones make up the cyber-world, in the same manner various combinations of matter and energy manifest themselves in the vast variety of the universe.

Role Of Matter And Energy

Matter, in one form or the other, is present everywhere in the universe. The earth, the stars, the space, all consist of and exist as matter. All organic or inorganic entitities, anywhere in the universe, represent one or the other form of matter. Form of matter at any point in time and space is determined by the forces which work on it at that point. No force can work independently of matter, for all energy is inherent in matter and no force can exist or operate in a vacuum. Neither matter nor energy can be created or destroyed; there are changes only in their form. Hydrogen combines with oxygen to form water. Water can take the form of ice or steam. But the quantity and the basic quality of the matter do not change. In other words, universe is a continuous flow of matter and energy, which has no beginning and no end. Since matter is being continually worked upon by force, the source of which resides in the matter itself, it is continually in flux.

Atom, which is at the heart of all matter and is regarded as made up of neutrons and electrons variously organized within and around a central nucleus, exhibits complex mass-energy characteristics. It admits of no division into smaller parts. Mass and energy cannot exist independently of each other, as the atom cannot be split into its mass and energy components. No gravitational force can be imagined without the existence of a particle of matter in which it is contained. The vice versa is equally true. No matter can exist without the inherent gravitational force. Any number of zeros and ones alone cannot create a binary system.

Different Forms Of Matter And Energy

In the terminology of physical science, matter exists in three forms, namely gaseous, liquid and solid, depending upon its density. Similarly, on the scale of intelligence capability, matter can be categorized as gross, fine and superfine, depending upon whether it can be worked upon by the *physical*, the *thought* or the *consciousness* force. Just as physical force works through gross matter and thought force works through fine matter, similarly consciousness force can present itself through superfine matter only. Fine and superfine matter can together be termed as mind-matter. However, all these divisions are temporary in nature. On physical as well as intelligence capability scale, matter can convert itself from one form into another. What are permanent are matter and the inherent energy, and not any of the forms. It is for this reason that the essential qualities of matter in any of its forms remain the same. The matter of the gross as well as the fine variety retains the basic qualities of the superfine matter. Similarly, physical and the thought energies both retain the basic qualities of the consciousness energy.

How It All Started

What is force? As per the dictionary meaning, force is an influence tending to cause movement. At one point in time, when creation had not manifested itself, all matter was lying in its inert form and all inherent energy existed in its potential form only. All matter existed in its superfine form and all energy was pure consciousness. It was the purest form of existence. It was formless, motionless and action less, and beyond the ambit of concepts of time and space. There was peace all around, as all forms of force were in equilibrium. At some stage when for some reason the equilibrium of the force was disturbed, the process of evolution started, which led to the creation. Part of the potential energy started converting itself into the kinetic energy and started working on the matter. As a result a chain reaction started, and formless matter started taking different forms, at different times and places. That is how stars, suns and spaces etc. came into being. From that moment onwards, concepts of time and space came into being. That is how the evolutionary process began, and continues ever since, and the consciousness started manifesting itself.

At this stage, there is movement all around, as the energy is continuously working on matter. In spite of the all-round movement, there is complete harmony and peace in the matter, for peace is the essential nature of matter-energy system. The only difference that the onset of evolution brought about was that static peace gave way to a dynamic peace. It is a dynamic peace because there is harmony in the interaction of matter and energy.

Origin Of Life

In spite of the fact that matter was taking different forms, which were changing every moment, there was no life at that stage of development. What is life? When physical energy works on gross matter, it is made to perform work. An object, made up of gross matter, may perform any amount of work under the influence of physical energy; it still remains an inorganic object. On the other hand, when matter in its fine form is worked upon by thought energy, it undergoes certain changes which impart to it the capability to do work or perform actions on its own. That is how life comes into being. Every thought wave, which carries with it the message of pleasure or pain, happiness or unhappiness, fear or fearlessness, fulfilment or inadequacy, and so on, produces specific changes in the matter being worked upon, and causes it to act accordingly. At the next stage of evolution, when the organic object performs action through the medium of consciousness energy, the object not only performs action but also becomes conscious of its own actions. That is how conscious life comes into being.

Why was there no life at the initial stage of evolution? Simply because the instrumentality of mind-body complex, through which life could express itself, had not evolved by that time. It came into existence at some stage, may be billions of years after the process of evolution started.

Thus life came into existence in the shape of an organic entity, having a body and a mind, when certain atoms of matter with their inherent energy combined and organized themselves into a functional unit. When this unit ceased functioning, it got reconverted into inorganic matter, leading to the death of the living organism. With passage of time, the organic entity, that is the mind-body complex, became more and more sophisticated. By and by, it added more and more functions to itself. It took birth, grew, decayed and in the end died. In between birth and death, it breathed. It felt hunger and thirst. It felt pleasure and pain. In short, it was a living being. However, at this stage, the organic being though alive was not conscious of its own existence. All functions of life were performed mechanically and instinctively, without exercising any choice.

This was the beginning of life in the universe. Earth may be only one of the places where life has evolved. It might have evolved at other places also. It might have evolved on different places at different times. It might be at initial stages of evolution at some places, whereas on others it may be in a more advanced stage. Moreover, instrumentality of life may be different at different places. Potential for the process of evolution is still unknown. At the present stage of evolution, it can only be visualized. It cannot be predicted. But one thing is sure. Destruction is as much part of the process of evolution as creation. But neither the creation nor the destruction refer to the matter or energy. Only the forms are created or destroyed. Matter and energy remain as they are.

It is possible that at some point of time in the future the manifestations of life may disappear. The equilibrium of the forces may be restored, and the energy may regain in its original form of pure consciousness. The cycle of existence as pure consciousness, manifestation of life and the return to the original form may have been repeated in the universe innumerable number of times.

Performance Of Action

Life, at the initial stages of development, existed in the form of primitive plants and animals of very low

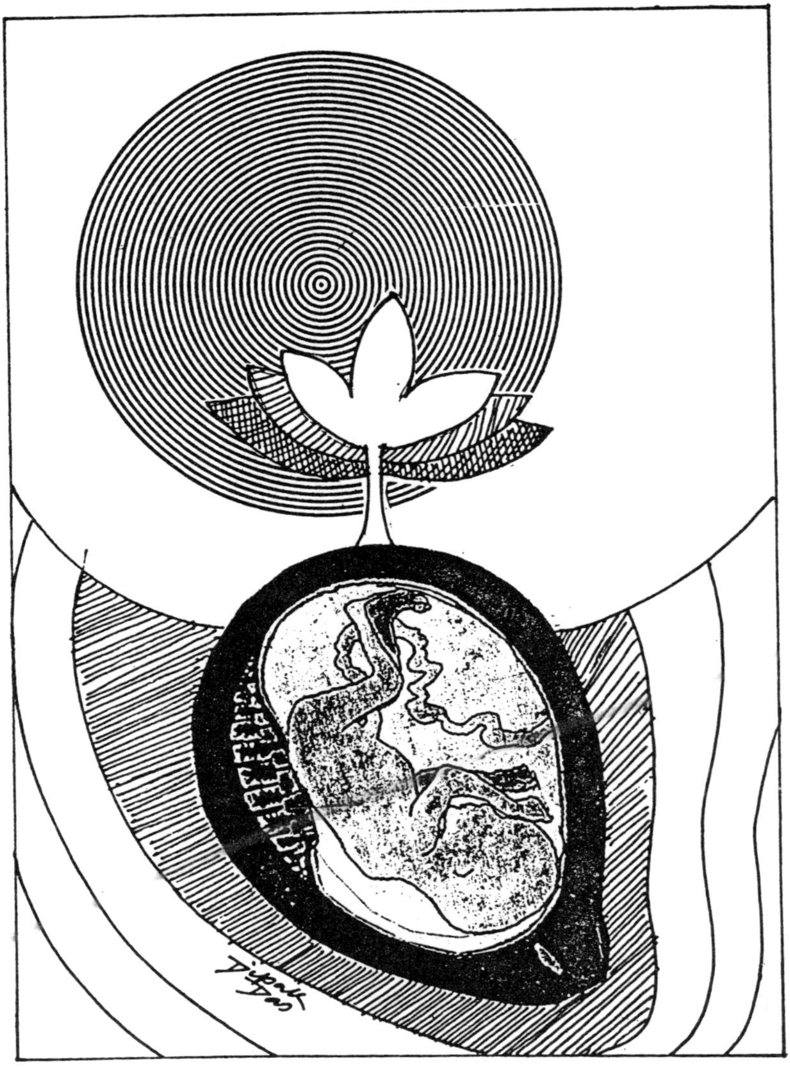
Dipak Das

intelligence. Further evolution led to the creation of more developed plants and highly intelligent animals. These animals were equipped with enough intelligence to make arrangements for their and their offspring's need for food, shelter, and protection from other animals etc. They even had societal life in as much as they lived in groups with well-defined rules. But they lacked in one important aspect. Even though they were doing whatever was required of them, they were doing it by instinct and in a mechanical fashion. They were not conscious of themselves - their own separate existence. The concept of ego was absent till that stage of development. Even till today, the more intelligent of the animals such as monkeys, chimpanzees or the more disciplined ones such as bees, ants etc., have no or very low sense of awareness, that is awareness of their own self.

Origin Of Conscious Life

Through continuous evolution, the body-mind complex acquired for itself the faculty of being aware or conscious. At this stage, small entities of gross, fine and superfine matter arranged as different mind-body complexes, energized by the physical and thought force, became aware not only of their own separate identity, but also of the separate identity of other entities. That is how the human being evolved.

Different Levels Of Existence

A human being, by definition, functions at three different levels, namely physical, intellectual and awareness level. These levels may also be referred to as body, mind and soul. These levels correspond to gross, fine and super-fine matter respectively on the one hand, and physical, thought and awareness energy on the other. The three levels, though separate and distinct, are inter-connected and inter-dependent. Superfine matter is only a finer form of fine matter, which in turn is a form of gross matter. Similar is the position with regard to different forms of energy.

Consciousness can express itself only through a mind and a body. Similarly, a mind can not be imagined without a physical instrument, that is the body through which it can function. In short, no higher-level existence can sustain itself without the support base of lower level existence. But at the same time, it cannot be denied that higher level of existence represents a more advanced stage in the evolutionary process. Thus human form is perhaps the best form evolved by nature so far. Enhancement of awareness on the part of human beings, at the individual as well as the collective level, can lead to an even better life, a life that would be more satisfying to the individual and more beneficial to the human society.

Performance Of Conscious Action

Awareness entails choice. Any conscious entity is not only entitled but also mandated to exercise choice every moment. Exercise of choice involves decision-making. Whereas every moment is the moment of choice for human beings, the animals usually act as they have been programmed to act by the nature. Decision-making by human beings leads to performance of conscious action. Even though animals also perform action, the quality of their action is different in-as-much as they are themselves not conscious of the same. It is just performed in a mechanical fashion. In the case of human beings, action is perceived to have been performed by oneself, that is a particular mind-body complex. The concept of oneself being separate from the universe and the performer of the action, is what can be termed an ego.

How The Ego Comes Into Being

If consciousness is the medium through which ego works, exercise of choice, decision-making and resultant performance of action are the catalysts which fortify the concept of ego. Every action contains in itself the seeds of its results. Action and its result are two sides of the same coin. The two cannot exist independent of each other. The chain of events, which form an integral part of life, is the culmination of numerous actions and their results. Since actions of individuals, all of whom have their own egos, affect these events, they imagine themselves to be the creators of those events, and not merely participants therein. They hold themselves as responsible for the happening or non-happening of specific events and experience the accompanying sensations of pleasure or pain. That is how the individual ego comes into being and gets reinforced every moment.

Aggregate Ego

As the individual ego evolves, simultaneously develops the concept of aggregate ego. Every individual ego is not only a separate entity in itself, it also forms part of various aggregate egos. An individual is part of a family, member of a religious group and citizen of a nation. All at the same time. Any aggregate ego is not a sum total of the individual egos. It has a personality and an identity of its own.

Notes

Being aware of one's strengths is not the same thing as inflation of ego, provided one is aware of one's weaknesses as well

Two

Nature of Ego

What is Ego

Individual ego is nothing but a momentary wave of thought in the vast ocean of consciousness. Such a wave arises in an independent unit of matter and its inherent energy i.e. mind-body complex. No individual ego can arise or survive in the absence of consciousness because ego is nothing but a thought, an idea, which can have no existence independent of consciousness. A stone, however huge, can have no idea about itself, an ego, as it is not working through the medium of consciousness. Similarly, an animal may only be rudimentarily conscious of itself and, hence, have no or very low ego. A human being, on the other hand, is conscious not only of himself but also about things and persons around him and accordingly has drawn a comparative picture of himself in his own mind that is called his ego. Ego is nothing but an image of one self as seen in the mirror of manifestation of consciousness. The comprehensive reality of consciousness is reflected in various fragmented forms through different mind-body complexes. Although it is a fact that no ego can arise in the absence of consciousness, it is equally true that no ego is possible without matter as ego arises only when energy in the form of thought works on matter in the form of body. The medium through which such an ego can arise is consciousness.

Micro And Macro Level Ego

There are two distinct ways in which an individual ego, a person, can view himself and other creatures. Firstly, it can be imagined that oneself is totally separate from and in competition with the remaining world. The other way of looking at things can be that one has no separate identity and represents one small facet of the whole creation for a moment. Both the ideas, though seemingly irreconciliable and representing two extremes, are two aspects of the same reality, which is the dynamic and omnipresent existence. These ideas represent the reality at micro and macro levels respectively. To use the cyber terminology again, when a computer operator functions at a micro level, he is aware just of his own machine; but when his awareness gets enhanced to a macro level, he sees himself as part of a network of machines. No person, at any point in time, can have only the micro level or the macro level ego. It has to be a combination of the two; but one ego may be predominant at one point of time and the other at another point of time. A person having micro level worldview can also be said to have an inflated ego as he considers himself to be the be all and end all of existence.

Whether a person at any given point of time has a micro dominant ego or a macro dominant ego depends mainly upon his present circumstances and past experiences. In addition to the circumstances and experiences, the will power of an individual also plays a major role in determining the nature of one's ego.

Dynamism of Ego

Every person is born with an ego, which is determined largely by the environment into which one is born and also the experiences one undergoes while still in the mother's womb. Ego is not a static concept but a dynamic and ever changing phenomenon, because it depends upon different constituents which themselves are never constant.

Role of Environment

The first and foremost impact on the self is of environment. No two individuals, being different, can share the same circumstances or the same environment. In some cases they can be similar but they can never be identical, not even in the case of twins. The environment of an individual is affected by numerous factors, one of them being one's location as measured on the scales of time and space. Time, by its very definition, never repeats itself. No moment of time, in whatever circumstances, comes back. As far as space is concerned, its infinite nature and also the fact that any atom of matter never remains static, makes it highly improbable for any atom of matter to come to the same point in space again and again. Thus, environment of an individual ego, which inter alia, depends upon the highly diverse and dynamic elements of time and space, is always in flux.

Role of Experience

Secondly, the role of experience. The experiences of an individual are contained in a metaphorical memory box, which consists of images of past happenings, actions performed, and the results thereof. For the sake of convenience, the memory box can be divided into two imaginary parts – one part containing the surface memory and the other the interior memory. These two parts correspond to what in common parlance are referred to as the conscious mind and the sub-conscious mind. Surface memory is the memory of which one is aware at any given point of time whereas interior memory is the memory which is hidden from the surface at that time. These two

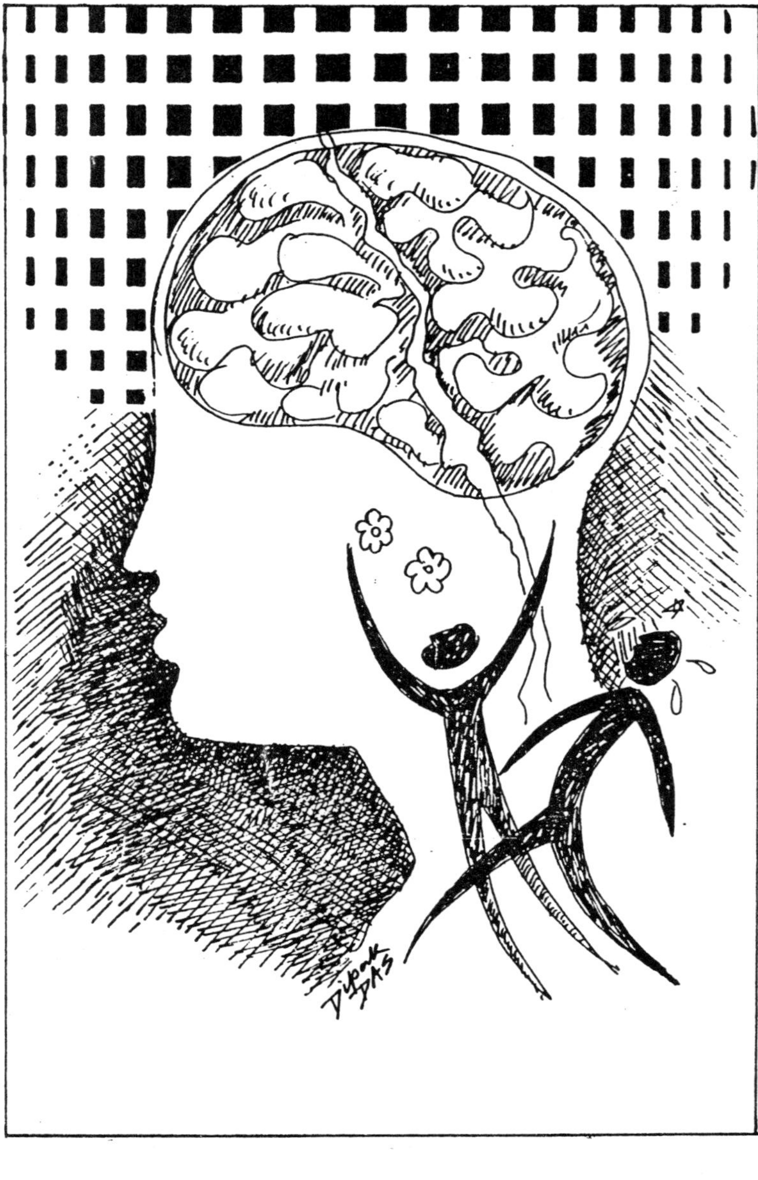

parts are not contained in two different watertight compartments. A long forgotten incident may come to surface in a moment and, on the other hand, a recent experience may be forgotten.

Role of Will power

The third and the most important factor that affects the ego is will power. The thought force, which operates through the mind matter, has a wonderful quality of controlling itself. In view of this quality, individual ego i.e. a person can be what he or she decides to be.

Thus, ego is a highly dynamic concept as it depends upon so many above mentioned factors, all of which are of a highly variable nature. However, it can arise and function only in the medium of consciousness.

Input and Output of Ego

There is another important aspect of ego, which needs special mention. Like other dynamic beings, ego feeds on an input and, in the process, generates an output. What does it consume and what does it produce? Ego, being a thought itself, survives on thought and its residue is also thought only. One of the most important determining factors of the quality of output of ego is the input fed to it.

An ego, which is fed on steroids such as false self-praise, flattery etc. ends up in frustration. On the other hand, those whose self-perception is based on the truth of life, lead a more contented life.

Rightful realization of the Ego

An inflated or bigger ego requires a bigger input, and generates, in turn, a bigger output. As such, a person having an inflated ego often comes into conflict with other persons, because in order to justify the volume of his ego, he has to claim credit for achievements which may be the result of hard work done by other people, and not by himself. At the same time, he has to deny responsibility for a failed action.

The real challenge is to right-size the ego. A deflated ego enters depression, insignificance. An inflated one, on the other hand, relates to the arena of the absurd as it loses touch with the reality. Right-sizing of ego can be achieved not by its measurement on a day-to-day basis, but by adopting right attitudes in life.

Ego and Pride

It needs to be clarified here that ego is not the same thing as pride. Where ego on the one hand refers to the quality of being conscious of oneself and being aware of its distinctiveness from the object of its thoughts and perceptions, pride relates to the sense of personal dignity and worth. Whereas the concept of ego tries to answer the oft-raised question 'what am I', pride replies the query as to 'how am I'.

To be proud of oneself is not an undesirable trait. It is rather essential for proper development of one's personality as one can genuinely be proud of one self only if he has some substantial achievement to his credit. Pride in oneself becomes reprehensible only when it degenerates into contempt for or indifference to others.

Notes

Every failure hides in itself the seeds of success,
Need is to find them;
And every success hides within it the seeds of failure,
They need be nipped in the bud;
Every success is the result of past efforts;
And every failure provides an opportunity for future improvement.

Three

How can the Ego be Managed

Managing one's ego is managing oneself. As per dictionary meaning, to manage is to direct, control or administer. To manage is not to conquer or subdue or vanquish. To manage also does not mean to appease. To manage one's ego is to direct one's affairs in such a manner as to serve the best interests of oneself and at the same time of the society at large. It must, here, be appreciated that interest of an individual need not necessarily be in conflict with the societal interest. They generally compliment each other.

Ego and the Self

The first and foremost requirement of managing any object is to have intimate knowledge of that object. For managing the ego well, one would have to have proper knowledge not only of the concept of ego but also of the self, of which it is an image. It must be understood at the outset that self of an individual is no different from comprehensive reality, that is the overall awareness. Whether any particular organic entity has no awareness, or a very low or a high degree of awareness at any given point of time, depends upon the capacity of its own instrument, that is mind-body complex at that time, to absorb and to interact with awareness. The fact of someone being low or high on the scale of awareness may affect its own self-perception but does not alter the essential character of the awareness itself. In a room, some objects may be more illuminated than others, but the nature of light itself does not vary from object to object. In the same manner, the nature of self, that is awareness or consciousness, does not change from person to person.

Self is the quality of being aware and also the substance of which it is aware. Ego, on the other hand, is the form of substance, that is, the self-image of which the mind-body complex is aware. The mind-body complex, simultaneously, is aware of other persons and objects as well.

Ego being an image, though distorted, of the self, it is most natural to compare the two. The Ego and the Self is perennial. It has always been and would always remain so, either in its pure form or the manifested one. It existed even when thought had not come into being. Ego, on the other hand, is momentary and the by-product of thought. It exists in the manifested form of self, and that too only when, and till some competent instrument in the shape of mind-body complex evolves and survives. Self on the one hand is a continuity, with no beginning and end, ego on the other is limited by the concept of time and space at the macro level, and by the mind and body at the micro level. The self represents the unchanging and comprehensive truth, whereas the truth represented by ego is temporary in nature, in-as-much as it lasts only till a particular body-mind complex survives. Self, by its very nature, can never change. It only changes its forms. On the other hand, ego is a dynamic concept. Constant change is its very nature. Self is beyond manipulation, whereas ego can be managed by hard and selfless work, and strong will-power.

Core Qualities of Ego and the Self

Does the ego converge, at some stage, with the self? To find a credible answer to this question, core qualities of both the ego and the self have to be understood and compared with each other. No person or an individual ego is comfortable with an unhappy state of mind. Everyone wants to be happy - always. Everyone also wants to be strong, healthy and at peace. From the above, it can safely be deduced that happiness, strength, peace and good health are the natural qualities of ego. Similarly, kindness is another quality, which forms the core of the ego. It is not to suggest that every person achieves the condition of being happy and strong etc. Far from it. But the fact that everyone strives for it and tries to get away from unhappiness indicates that negative aspects of life are foreign to the uncorrupted form of ego.

The more an individual ego experiences happiness, strength etc. in one's life, the more it reflects the true image of self. As a matter of fact, when one realizes oneself to be nothing else but happiness, strength, peace, good health and kindness, one reflects the true image of self and, in a way, merges with it. At this stage, one enjoys most satisfying material and spiritual life.

Then the question arises as how to realize this truth. For any sort of realization, first step is to acquire knowledge of that subject. But having a mere theoretical knowledge of truth does not ensure its realization. Because knowledge can penetrate directly only the conscious mind, whereas a major portion of human mind relates to the sub-conscious.

How can the knowledge of truth be made to pierce the metaphorical veil of ignorance separating the conscious from the sub-conscious mind? For this purpose, a comparative study of these two parts of the human mind will have to be conducted. But before that is even

attempted, it is essential to understand the overall nature of body and mind.

Nature of Body and Mind

Body is not the final product. Otherwise it would have stopped growing or deteriorating at a particular point in time. The atoms of matter, which constitute one particular body at any moment, are not same at any other moment. At least some of them are necessarily different. It is an ever evolving process. Since the atoms, different at different times, are organized in a particular fashion, they give an impression of continuity. Human or for that matter any other body is not a product but a process. Human mind, on the other hand, is the continuity of never-ending waves which arise in the sea of thought and awareness energy. These two forms of energy interact with the fine and superfine portions of matter respectively, which form part of the human body. Thought and awareness process which relates to a particular body, survives till the body survives. Both conscious and sub-conscious varieties of mind interact with each other and the body continuously.

The Conscious and the Sub-conscious Mind

What is the nature of similarities and dissimilarities between the conscious and the sub-conscious mind? The conscious mind is the continuous stream of thought waves of which one is conscious at any point in time. The sub-conscious mind, on the other hand, is the sum total of recordings of experiences and legacies of experiences through which one has undergone. From conception till death, every human being goes through different experiences. But what are legacies of experiences?

Life, in a way, can be described as a chain of events in which every organic and inorganic being participates. Inorganic objects have no faculty which can have a sense of participation, and the organic objects other than human beings participate without any or very low sense of participation. However, the human beings not only have a sense of participation but also a sense of creation with respect to these events. The occurrence of events has a logic of its own, as it is the result of actions performed or abstained by various organic and inorganic beings. An entity can have influence on events occurring at a particular place and time even if it is not present at that place and at that point of time.

Every independent entity participates in and influences this chain of events, but it is only organic beings who can experience some of these events. Since the individual ego, being aware of itself and of the events, identifies itself with some of these events, not as a mere participant but as a creator thereof, it develops a liking or dislike for a particular event depending upon whether it feels pleasure or pain on the occurrence of that event. It develops feelings of like or dislike even for objects and persons associated with these events. Due to the individual likes and dislikes, one tries to manipulate the events as per one's liking. At times one may succeed, and at times one may not. But in no case does one succeed all the time, because any event, being part of an infinite chain, is the result of an interplay of innumerable forces released by the actions performed or abstained by various organic and inorganic entities. Including, of course, the actions or non-actions of the individual concerned. Since ego considers itself to be the creator and not merely a participant of events, it holds itself responsible for achieving or failing to achieve the desired results. That is how every experience, that is participation in an event, creates its own legacy.

The above discussion tries to throw some light on the nature of the conscious and the sub-conscious mind. Whereas one is the name given to current thought process going on in an individual's mind matter, the other is sum total of its experiences and their after-effects. To word it differently, sub-conscious part is the 'recording room' of the mind, which keeps a record of not only the events experienced by the individual, but also of the accompanying feelings. The intensity of these feelings can be substantially reduced if one is aware of the intrinsic nature of the chain of events while undergoing any of these experiences.

How do the two compare with each other in other aspects? Conscious mind is a small fraction of the total mind. Major portion of the total mind is of the sub-conscious variety which keeps on increasing as the age of an individual advances. Whereas the conscious mind is guided by reason and logic depending upon the knowledge and intelligence of an individual, the thoughts generated by the past experiences and their legacies lie in a most anarchic fashion in the sub-conscious mind. Since the conscious mind is guided by reason and logic, it is amenable to discipline. The sub-conscious mind, on the other hand, can't be so controlled. It rather interferes with orderly functioning of the conscious mind.

To put it in a broader frame, a human being enjoys the fruits of life in this world through the agency of body and mind in the medium of awareness. Life becomes a pleasure if all the three i.e. body, mind and awareness work in harmony. Of the three, awareness is the constant factor as its basic nature is the same everywhere. Of the remaining two, mind is the most dynamic concept. As far as human body is concerned, it is the result of a process of evolution spread over billions of years. It can take care of itself in every respect but only if not grossly mishandled. But no harmonious life is possible without a healthy body. Thus the part of one's personality which is most difficult to handle, due to its inherent dynamism, is the mind. The mind, as discussed earlier, consists of two parts. As the

conscious mind is governed by reason, it is not difficult to manage it. The past experiences, which form part of the sub-conscious mind, are a great help in analyzing the current situations and taking correct decisions.

Legacies of Experiences

The other part of the sub-conscious mind, namely the legacies of experiences, which are not amenable to reason, are the most difficult to manage. As discussed earlier, the legacies arise due to the misinterpretation by the individual ego of its role in the occurrence of chain of events. When an event provides comfort to the mind-body complex of an individual ego, it develops a liking for that event. Without realizing that every event is only a link in the never-ending chain of events and, therefore, is the result of various known and unknown forces, one gives credit to oneself. Accordingly, one gets a feeling of satisfaction. However, such a feeling of satisfaction is very short-lived, for it is overtaken by a feeling of fear whether the subsequent events would bring similar results or not. Similarly, a feeling of dissatisfaction arises when any event leads to discomfort to the mind-body complex, and this feeling in turn is responsible for the feeling of guilt, because the ego holds itself responsible for the unsatisfactory results.

Thus, fear and guilt are the basic legacies that get generated from time to time in the sub-conscious mind of an individual. Depending upon a particular situation, these feelings present themselves in various forms such as greed, jealousy and anger etc.

There is constant interaction between logic i.e. conscious mind and experiences contained in the sub-conscious mind, on the one hand, and the legacies of the sub-conscious, on the other. More often than not, logic is overshadowed by the legacies. That is why, driven by the

past legacies, many a time, one grows confused, even with wide open eyes. Not all legacies are equally strong. But each and every legacy influences the conscious mind according to its own potency. In managing one's ego i.e. oneself, the biggest challenge is to rein in these legacies, and to realize the real self.

How can the Legacies be managed

How can that be accomplished? No one can prescribe any exclusive manner of accomplishment. There can be as many ways as the numbers of human beings, because everyone has to search for the truth of life in his own way. Any method which helps in reducing the accretion of legacies and neutralizing the existing ones, and in understanding the truth that one is nothing but happiness, strength, peace and kindness, is the right method. This knowledge can be made to penetrate the sub-conscious portion of mind in various ways such as through meditation, selfless work for others, complete surrender before the forces of nature etc. None of these methods is exclusive. They are, in fact, complimentary to each other.

What is meditation?

Meditation can be described as a process of becoming more and more aware of the chain of thoughts which continuously go on in one's mind-matter and also of the resultant-action-result syndrome. Such sharpening of awareness can be achieved in many ways, and not necessarily by sitting in a particular posture or by constantly reciting some mantra etc. To clearly understand the concept of meditation, it is necessary to understand that at the back of one's mind, there always goes on an involuntary chain of thoughts, over which one has no control. This chain of thoughts is prompted by past legacies, and continues to trouble the individual, whether he is performing some work or is just relaxing. A simple

and positive thought when employed persistently can help the individual in converting this involuntary chain of thoughts, which otherwise is a drag on his satisfaction level and capacity to perform, into a voluntary and positive thought process which would be in consonance with the work being performed. The thought process can be given a right direction only by first becoming aware of it and then convincing oneself that it can be controlled by strong will power. Positive thought process, being more orderly, consumes less energy. The thought and consequently the physical energy, so conserved, can then be utilized for improving one's quality of life.

Selfless Work

Selfless work does not mean work without any aim, purpose or planning. It also does not mean work only for others and without any benefit for oneself. Nor does it mean work beyond one's capacity. Selfless dedicated work, on the other hand, is well planned and executed work, keeping one's own interest and also the interest of the society at large in view, and at the same time being aware of the fact that the result of one's actions does not depend solely upon one's actions but on various other factors also. Constant knowledge of the nature of occurrence of events insulates oneself from the results of one's actions. By and by, one understands that work is its own best reward. Similarly, the concept of complete surrender cannot be an excuse for non-action. It is, in fact, a way of living where all worries and fears are left to the Lord and fresh energy is received every moment from the same source. One surrenders oneself completely before the forces of nature with the knowledge, belief and confidence that they are never biased against anyone.

How do such techniques work? While one is performing action without bothering about its results or is engaged in any one of the above or similar activities, one's conscious mind gets calm, as one is not worried about the results. Accordingly, mental activity at the conscious level is reduced. Thus a partial or near total, as the case may be, vacuum is created in the conscious part of mind. Nature abhors vacuum. In such a situation, legacies lying hidden in the cavities of sub-conscious mind come to the surface i.e. in the region of consciousness. Thus the legacies, instead of indirectly affecting the thought process of a person, enter directly the realm of awareness. If one does not react to these legacies they get burnt up in the fire of awareness and thus get neutralized. This theory can be questioned on the ground as to why legacies do not appear and get neutralized during sleep, when there is almost no mental activity at the conscious level. It is true that during sleep also the legacies appear on surface. In fact, they manifest themselves in the form of dreams. But there is no question of their getting neutralized then as the medium of awareness is absent at that stage.

Need for Strong Will power

In the fight against legacies, strong will-power i.e. firm determination to win is a potent weapon in the hands of logic. Will-power, in fact, is the win-power which needs to be strengthened from time to time.

When legacies get neutralized, logic and experience work in unison freely in the medium of awareness. Only then can one realize the true meaning of life. Neutralization of legacies helps in another manner also. In the normal course of events, a lot of not only mental but also physical energy is lost due to struggle between logic and the legacies. When legacies get weakened, part of such energy gets saved and can be put to better use. By neutralizing legacies, one can also put one's time to better use. If one analyses use of one's time dispassionately, it would be clearly seen that a major part of one's time is spent either rueing about the past or worrying about the future. Enhanced awareness can certainly help in avoiding such a situation. One can learn to live in the present. One can live every moment of life.

But it is not sufficient to neutralize the legacies. It also needs to be ensured that there are no fresh accumulations. Such accumulations can be avoided by understanding the true nature of life and working accordingly.

The role of legacies in human behaviour can be better appreciated by observing the behaviour of a small child. Why are the reactions of a child so instant, so innocent and so intense? Simply because the experiences undergone and therefore the legacies accumulated by the child are very limited. The accumulation, being not very large, is not in a position to overpower the logic of conscious mind. Thus the child reacts to a situation without much reference to previous experiences and legacies, that is, it reacts to the prevalent circumstances and not to the circumstances as they could have been, would have been or should have been. That is why it weeps inconsolably when it is hurt and laughs heartily when it feels like laughing.

Role of Society

Working of the human mind can also be understood in a slightly different but more simplistic manner. Man is supposed to be born free, but is conceived to be everywhere in chains. It is difficult to imagine a human being who, from day one, is not tied to the strings of family, financial status, religion, state and other similar affiliations. In fact, many a time, one's very existence is defined by one or more of such limitations.

Every affiliation puts forward a set of demands on one's social behaviour, resulting in suppression of innumerable desires and other feelings. A feeling can be suppressed but it cannot be eliminated. Hence, the suppressed desires and other controlled feelings, though not visible on surface, form an integral but troublesome part of one's personality.

When one starts practicing introspection and learns to analyse one's own thought-processes dispassionately, one comes face to face with such hidden emotions. At this stage if one does not react to such emotions and faces them with equanimity, they lose their potency and thus potential for trouble. Slowly and slowly junk gets cleared, and it becomes possible for one to attain a state of mind where both peace and progress can be attained simultaneously.

Role of Human Body

In addition to what has been discussed above, it has also to be understood that a healthy mind can flourish only in a healthy body. If any part of one's body is in pain, it becomes very difficult to create a vacuum in the conscious mind and to give a chance to the legacies to expend themselves. As the body affects the mind, so does the mind affect the body. A healthy mind helps the body to be disease-free. Even a small but persistent and strong thought can help in rejuvenating the whole human system. If one can genuinely convince oneself that his real self is nothing but awareness, which consists of happiness, peace, strength and kindness themselves, one can surely experience such a state of mind in due course of time. Not only that. Even some instant result can also be experienced.

In short, by performing action without much expectation, and at the same time by keeping the legacies of experiences in check, one can, through enhanced awareness, manage oneself well, and thereby lead a personally satisfying and socially beneficial life.

Notes

Dread not the death
For it is only another form of life
Dread instead the vacuum—the state
of having nothing more to do
For it is the very negation of life.

Four

Relationship Of Part To The Whole

Laws of Nature

The existence - anything that exists anywhere including space and vacuum - is governed by a set of rules, which can be called laws of nature. Everything, everyone and every event forms part of a system. There is nothing which may be visualized outside the system. Every part of the system, howsoever big or small, is bound by these principles. These laws, which govern the entire universe, apply to all entities within it equally and without exception. They would cease to be laws if they admitted of any differentiation or partiality. Further, since the system is all encompassing, there can be no outside agency controlling or influencing the system. It is a self-governing arrangement.

Dynamism is the cardinal principle of this system. Even the smallest unit of matter and energy, the atom, is never static. Nothing ever is permanent; neither the stars and the planets, nor life with the accompanying feelings and experiences of living beings.

Three Categories

Seen through the partially open window of human knowledge at a particular point of time, laws of nature can

Dipak Das

be broadly divided into three categories. In the first category are laws that the humanity knows for certain, such as the fact that whosoever is born, has to die. The laws established by physical sciences also belong to this category. In the second category are those phenomena of nature about which man speculates and hypothesises without being certain, such as those in the fields of astrology. Lastly, there are facts and laws about which humanity is totally in the dark, in spite of phenomenal progress made in the fields of physical and social sciences. These facts and laws are unknown today, even though the light of human knowledge may illuminate some of them in the future.

The System

This division is relevant only in the limited context of human perception, for the universe itself is one integrated whole and does not admit of any division. The universe is in itself the subject and object of knowledge. The concepts of time and space serve only to define a particular facet of nature. As stated earlier, nature is a perfectly functional system. It is indivisible. By corollary, laws which form part of and govern the system are also indivisible. The system, however, consists of various sub-systems which though otherwise full-fledged operational systems in themselves cannot survive independently. The solar system is one such example. Human body is another.

The Sub-systems and the Other Smaller Systems

These sub-systems, in turn, comprise of numerous sub-subsystems, which are further formed by smaller and smaller systems. If the solar system, of which earth is a part, is taken as an example, solar system is a sub-system of which earth is a sub-subsystem. Similarly, respiratory system, digestive system and nervous system are smaller systems of the human body. An atom, probably, is the

smallest known sub-system of mass and energy which is a fully functional system in itself.

In other words, every entity in the universe functions in accordance with certain rules. Whereas inorganic entities perform their functions without any sense of involvement therein, organic beings not only perform actions voluntarily but also hold themselves responsible for their results depending upon the level of consciousness achieved by them. The consciousness level achieved by an individual organic entity depends not only upon the species to which it belongs but also upon it own endeavours.

The Truth

Even though the universal system is constituted by various sub-systems and innumerable smaller systems, it is not a sum total of all the constituent systems, just as human body is not a mere aggregation of the body organs. It has a personality of its own. It has a mind of its own. It is the cosmic cycle, the universal system. This is the Reality. This is the Truth - an unchanging existence with an ever-changing face. Call it Nature, the Truth, God or whatever. By its very definition, existence is omnipresent. It cannot, however, be described as omnipotent, as it is bound by its own rules. It has for instance evolved a system for a chicken to come out of an egg, but it cannot put it back into the egg. From the above discussion, it also follows that God is one. To suggest otherwise would be ridiculous. It is another matter that in accordance with their understanding, different individuals and communities may describe or depict Him in different words and images.

Fuel and Exhaust of the system

No dynamic system, be it organic, mechanical, electronic or any other, can function without an input, or the fuel, as it were. It also generates an output, which may be referred to as the exhaust. A human being, or for that matter any living organism, cannot survive without the inputs of air, water and food. Excretion of waste is equally necessary for its survival. Similarly, no machine can work without consuming a fuel and generating an exhaust. The exhaust of one system often serves as the fuel of the other. Thus, systems, sub-systems and other smaller systems created by the evolutionary process compliment as well as supplement each other. But they cannot function independently, because they are dependent upon other systems for the supply of their fuel and absorption of their exhaust. Thus, none of them can be called perfect.

The only exception to this is the universal system. It is a perfect system because it does not depend upon any other agency for its survival. It generates its own fuel and absorbs its own exhaust. This system being all encompassing, no agency outside its scope can even be visualized. Thus only Nature or Truth or God, whatever name we may give to it, is perfect. All else is imperfect and incomplete.

Of all the individual entities, only human beings, due to the structure of their body and mind, are in a position to visualize the Truth. Therefore, only human beings, even though they may be a small part of the whole gamut of existence, can relate to the Whole. This relationship can be based either on the knowledge of the Truth, or upon fear of the unknown.

Fear of the Unknown

'Fear of the Unknown' leads to the establishment of obscure beliefs, dogmas and rituals. This situation is generally exploited by the so-called godmen, prophets and self-proclaimed sons and daughters of the God. Knowledge of the Truth, on the other hand, leads to the realization of oneself being nothing else but happiness, peace, strength and kindness. Such a realisation establishes one in a state of mind which can only be described as a state of bliss.

Realisation of the Truth

True knowledge has to be realised directly, and not through hear-say or any messengers. Each individual has to select his own path to the realisation of knowledge and then traverse it. In other words, truth has not only to be believed but also personally realised. If truth is to be realised, it has to be first understood as to what is the main obstacle to its realisation. As discussed earlier, legacies of experiences act as hurdles in realising the truth through rational thought and logical action. One way to overcome this hurdle would be to eliminate one's likes and dislikes so that the cause of genesis of the legacies is removed. However, it is a tall order. One is bound to develop likes and dislikes for events, objects and persons depending upon whether they provide comfort or discomfort to one's mind-body complex. What is required is not the curbing of the desire or of the likes and dislikes, but to check the accumulation of legacies of experiences. Thus, one may have likes and dislikes and fully participate in the events, but at the same time take care not to let the legacies overpower logic. In other words, one raises the level of one's awareness. This is the better way to realise the truth.

Knowledge vs Awareness

Awareness, in fact, is the key to the realisation of Truth. It may here be re-iterated that awareness is not the same thing as knowledge. Whereas knowledge refers to information or understanding about objects, events or persons including about one's own self, awareness relates to the one who has acquired this information or understanding. Unless tempered with awareness, knowledge tends to breed arrogance. And the arrogance of knowledge is more dangerous than the curse of ignorance.

Awareness is the medium through which one can understand oneself. Awareness is the ray of light which can illuminate the darkest cavities of life. Thus, to understand truly one's relationship with the Creator, one has to be aware of oneself always. One has to be aware of one's thoughts, actions, the results of actions and of the entire unending chain of events. One has to be aware of one's strengths and weaknesses, of one's past and current experiences and the legacies arising out of them; of one's pleasures and pains. One has also to stay alert that none of them is permanent. One has to be aware of one's environment and of other organic and inorganic entities. One has to be aware of all aspects of life, always. To step up the level of awareness, one has to think about what one is doing and to do what one is thinking about. Small but persistent steps in this direction can bring about dramatic improvement in one's achievement graph. Mind and body function more logically and systematically when they are under constant observation by the self. Thus, by being aware, a lot of psychosomatic disorders can be prevented and even cured.

Living In the Third Person

When one begins to look at oneself as one looks at others, and the 'you-and-me' regime changes into the 'he-and-he' regime, then one starts analysing one's own mistakes in the same manner as one does those of others. At this stage, the truth of existence starts revealing itself to the individual, because he starts seeing the world from a broader perspective of the self instead of the narrow angle of ego. Instead of looking at the world just through the prism of intellect, one looks at it under the light of the awareness as well. Then the part falls into complete harmony with the whole. All tensions and discords melt in

Dipak Das

the fire of awareness, because the incorrect interpretation of ego, which is the source of all these tensions and discords, gets exposed. Thus, one has to be aware of one's breathing, of one's walking. In short, one has to be aware of whatever one does or does not do. Awareness is a perfect antidote to living an instinctive and mechanical life. It is the only medium which separates the human beings from other organic creatures. It is, in fact, the essence of human life. One has to be aware always. By stepping up the level of awareness, one can realize the truth of the whole system of which one is a small, but vital, part.

To use a simple analogy, one can be described as an infinite reservoir of matter and energy. If one acquires true knowledge about Him, and devotes all one's actions to Him and accepts the results thereof as His grace, one can establish unity with god, and can thereafter draw as much energy from this reservoir as one is capable of absorbing. That is how a part realizes itself to be an integral and inseparable part of the whole.

Notes

Sin against God is no different from a crime against humanity And a neglect of oneself too

Five

Exception to the Rule

As discussed in the preceding chapter, every thing, every one and every event is governed by an all-pervasive and defined set of rules. Similarly, the result of actions performed or left unperformed by an individual or aggregate entities are determined by laws, which are totally impartial.

These laws are broadly known to everyone, but their intricacies often remain hidden due to lack of awareness on the part of entities which are subject to these laws. Lack of awareness of the true nature of these laws often leads to a false perception that there are exceptions to these rules.

An Illusion

An individual or an aggregate ego, while performing action, creates an illusion that it can escape the undesirable results of its actions because every rule has an exception. One thinks that rules of nature are applicable to everyone, but he himself would be saved by the perceived exception. Such an illusion is stronger in the case of a micro dominant ego.

Enhanced awareness helps one to understand that exception to rules of nature is nothing else but an illusion. If at all there is any exception to any rule of nature, such exception itself is governed by some other rule. Laws of nature are perfect only because they are impartial. To illustrate, if anger affects the metabolism of a person in a particular manner, it must affect every person in the same manner. There is no way anyone can escape the after-effects of anger, even though they may not be immediately visible due to the observer's ignorance. This creates the illusion of exception to the rule, which is actually not there.

Thus, whereas an egoistic person performs actions under the belief that the adverse results of his actions would not befall him, an aware person knows the consequences of his actions, and therefore corrects them even before actually executing them.

Notes

Prayer does not changes things
It only changes one's perception about them

Six

Vicious Circle Vs. The Virtuous Spheroid

How One Gets Caught in A Vicious Circle

A great majority of us, most of the times, think in one manner, but act in another. A chain smoker knows for certain that smoking is harmful for health, decides to leave it, and promises to himself and his well-wishers that he would not touch it again; but the very next moment he smokes even more vigorously. How and why does it happen? Why does rational thought often get defeated in the battle against irrationality? As has been discussed in the earlier chapters, legacies of past experiences usually prove more powerful than logic, and as a result rational thought gets over-ruled. Irrational thought leads to irrational action. Such illogical actions, by their very nature, produce undesirable results. Since these actions and their results arise out of ignorance and result in momentary pleasure and pain, they generate their own legacies. In the process, the earlier legacies get reinforced. Thus, legacies become stronger and stronger and in turn instigate more and more illogical thought and action. That is how one gets caught in a vicious circle.

How to get out of it? Before any sincere effort is made to answer this question, it has to be examined if majority of us do really want to get out of this vicious circle. The answer appears to be obvious but it is actually not so. We become accustomed to this type of living, irrespective of the fact that it results in more pain than pleasure. In a way, we develop a fondness for the vicious circle which may lead to a miserable life. This is mainly because we have not known any alternative - a different way of living.

An Alternative

Before any sincere effort is made to break the vicious circle, one has to explore the possible alternatives. Is there an alternative way of living? Is there a way of living whereby one can participate in worldly affairs to one's maximum capacity without accumulating any ill-effecting legacies of one's actions? In view of what I have said so far, an alternative method of living is not only possible, but should also be one of the most satisfying and enjoyable experience. When one performs action under an enhanced awareness, one understands the true nature of action and its results, and therefore the actions do not generate any legacies. In such a situation one realises one's real nature, which is made up of nothing but happiness, peace, strength and kindness. As a result, one breaks the vicious circle and enters a virtuous spheroid.

How To Get Out of The Vicious Circle

Since the vicious circle in which one gets caught, is of one's own making, methods have to be devised to get out of it by oneself only. Others can only suggest different possible ways. Thus, one has to first of all recognize that one is caught in a vicious circle, that it is possible to come out of it, and that an excellent alternative is available. Thereafter one has to make a determined bid to get out of it by choosing a path for this purpose and steadfastly treading on it. But, a word of caution. Path here does not refer to any exclusive, complicated and mysterious method of achieving any so-called salvation of the soul; it refers

Dipak Das

merely to a simple and positive way of living, through which one may realize the truth of existence, and thereby lead a useful, happy and satisfying life.

Methods of Escape: Evolutionary And Revolutionary Processes

Breaching the forte of vicious circle of legacies can be attempted in two ways, which are not necessarily mutually exclusive. First method of breaking the hold of legacies arises out of an evolutionary process; and the second course is the result of a revolutionary event. Of the two methods, the revolutionary event that changes the entire course of one's life is a rare occurrence. Only legendary figures like Valmiki or Tulsidas can transform themselves completely due to the happening of an event. Such people suddenly break free from the circle of legacies, and automatically enter the virtuous spheroid. But lesser mortals have to virtually slog it out through the process of evolution.

Evolution, by its very nature, is a slow process. Every human being, at a given point of time, functions at a certain level of awareness. Through will power, which consists of qualities of determination, observation and concentration etc., one can enhance this level of awareness. How can the will power be strengthened? When one does what one decides to do and decides to do what one is capable of doing, will-power gets strengthened, slowly and slowly. Strong will power leads to enhanced awareness, which is the most potent weapon for breaking the vicious circle of legacies.

Awareness, being the quality of being aware, is always present everywhere in an infinite form. Enhancement of awareness means enhancement of the capacity of mind-body complex of a particular individual to become more aware of himself and his surroundings. Mind-body complex of each organic entity has some capacity to interact with awareness, which is mainly determined by the species to which the particular entity belongs. Insects may have almost nil awareness. Monkeys have much more. But it is only human beings who can clearly visualize themselves and others as 'I', 'You', ' It', 'He' etc. They can not only contemplate abstract ideas such as God, Nature, etc., but are also aware of their relationship with them. Even though the capacity of humans to absorb awareness is substantial, it is not unlimited. It is limited by the structure of their mind-body complex, that is, by the capacity of their five sense organs on the one hand, and by the limitations of a particular thought process on the other. Beyond the capacity of mind-body complex, it is pure awareness.

But within the limits set by nature, there is a lot of scope for enhancing one's awareness level.

Role of Awareness

How does awareness work? Mind-matter, through the instrumentality of human body, experiences pleasure and pain. In the process, ego attaches itself to this pleasure and pain syndrome and suffers the resultant consequences. Through enhanced awareness, on the other hand, one can understand the true nature of pleasure and pain. One can also appreciate that pleasure and pain give rise to likes and dislikes. The feeling of fear and guilt, which present themselves in various forms such as anger, greed at different times, are derivatives of such likes and dislikes. Enhanced awareness further helps one to understand that various derivatives of likes and dislikes keep on multiplying in the darkness of ignorance. In fact, one understands that ignorance begets ignorance and legacies beget legacies. Under the bright light of enhanced awareness, one starts analysing the reasons for such multiplication, and at the same time starts checking it. Continuous enhanced awareness starts eradicating such derivatives i.e. legacies of various experiences. Awareness begets awareness and happiness begets happiness. That is how an effective attack is made on the vicious circle of legacies.

Enhanced awareness helps in bridging the gap between the world of perception, which is the domain of knowledge, and the world of reality, which expresses itself through the medium of awareness.

Virtuous Spheroid

When one gets out of the vicious circle, even momentarily, one automatically enters, in that moment, an area that can only be described as virtuous spheroid, for during this period one perceives oneself to be happy, peaceful, strong and kind, and is not troubled by fear, guilt, anger etc. In these moments, one does not have to make and break determinations from time to time. One does not have to seek happiness. One experiences a state of joyfulness without any special effort or reason. Purification of mind improves the quality of sleep as well.

Let it be examined how the vicious circle gets transformed into a virtuous spheroid under the influence of enhanced awareness. Enhanced awareness helps one in understanding that one is a small but vital part of Nature. Thus the gap between the two, that is between oneself and Nature, which is created due to wrong perceptions of the individual, gets narrowed down. One, in fact, can attain complete oneness with Nature. In such a situation, one perceives Nature not as an adversary but as a complimentary force. Relationship established is that of a Creator and His creation. Nature being perceived to be on one's side, one attains supreme confidence in oneself and as a consequence in the others around. Such confidence eliminates fear from one's heart and helps in transforming the vicious circle into a virtuous spheroid.

Breaking the circle once is not enough. It has to be a continuous process as the mind-matter is under constant pressure of the inherent gravitational force of other objects and events. Thus, even after breaking the vicious circle for some time, one again falls in the same trap and in the process forgets oneself. Strong will power and sustained effort can establish oneself in awareness, so that even while performing actions with full vigour, one is not troubled by the past, and is also not concerned about the results. Awareness helps not only in understanding oneself, but also in leading a more purposeful and satisfying worldly life. Thus, one enters a virtuous spheroid where one can overcome the surface tension and realize peace deep inside. Turbulence of the surface can be understood only after one has experienced the calmness of the deep sea. Awareness, by enabling one to understand one's real nature, leads to a happier life. One realizes that happiness, strength, peace and kindness are essential ingredients not only of oneself, but also of the life cycle, as a whole.

It must be emphasized, here, that a virtuous spheroid is not some distant, mysterious or theoretical concept. Any one with a reasonable degree of determination and effort can attain a state of mind where nothing would ever go wrong.

Notes

Aware relationships do not bind

Seven

Web of Relationships

So far, we have seen in the preceding chapters that an individual entity, be it organic or inorganic, has been looked into as an aware or unaware participant in the perennial chain of events. But there is another angle from which the existence of every creature can be examined. No one can function in a vacuum. Everyone is related to everyone else in one way or the other.

Life, in a way, can be described as an infinite web of numerous visible and invisible relationships established among different organic and inorganic objects. Any number of points, unless joined together, cannot create a web. Similarly, no life cycle can be sustained for long unless entities are joined with each other through the strings of relationships. Not only that. Continuity of existence is maintained through the complex networking of the past, present and the future relationships.

A Multi-dimensional Concept

Life is not unidimentional. Web of relationships, which is one of the most important determining factors of life, also falls into the same category. Every individual member of the web, at any point in time, enters into different relationships with the other members and consequently performs various roles simultaneously. A human being, for example, may be a citizen of a nation, a member of a

religious group, a father, a son, a doctor – all at the same time. Demands of different relationships at times appear to be contradictory to each other. Art of living lies in balancing the responses to different demands.

Dynamism of Relationships

No relationship between two human beings, or for that matter between any two different creatures, can ever be static because the creature itself is a dynamic concept. Life is another name given to dynamism. A relationship is an ever-changing and ever-evolving phenomenon. Even the relationships which are seemingly stable, keep on changing their shades and evolving continuously. A mother-child relationship is no exception. For the first few months of its existence, the infant identifies itself completely with its mother. It has no independent identity in its own eyes. But as the child grows 'aware', the love-love relationship takes different shades of the love-anger relationship, the love-hate relationship etc. Dynamism represents the beauty as well as the essence of relationships. Challenge of life lies in understanding this dynamism of relationships and adjusting one's behaviour accordingly.

Relationship with Abstract Ideas

As discussed earlier, an independently identifiable entity establishes some sort of visible or invisible relationship with other entities. Whereas in inorganic creatures such relationships are determined by circumstances, the organic beings, in addition to the relationships inherited by circumstances, establish relationships by instinct as well as by choice. Among the organic creatures also, only the aware beings are capable of establishing relationships with abstract concepts such as God, a nation, a religious group etc. These concepts are abstract not because they are less important than concrete entities, but because they cannot be experienced in a direct manner by the five sense organs provided by Nature to the human beings. They can only be felt at heart. An abstract relationship can be as strong and important as a relationship between any concrete entities.

Rights and Duties

Every relationship requires a role to be played by the entities involved in that relationship. Every role, in turn, bestows a privilege upon the person performing that role. But the privilege of a role depends not only upon the role itself but also upon the manner in which it is performed. But no privilege can survive in a vacuum. Every privilege is invariably accompanied by a corresponding responsibility. Duty, in fact, is inherent in any right itself. Neither of the two can have an independent existence.

Every relationship need not necessarily be a reciprocal relationship, but a purely give-give or a purely take-take relationship cannot sustain itself for long.

Unfortunately, due to a lack of understanding of the true nature of relationships, sometimes the relationships themselves as well as the roles played as a consequence thereof get distorted. Emphasis is laid on one aspect of the relationship at the cost of the other. Sometimes, relationships which provide momentary materialistic gains are given more weightage than the long-term human relationships. On some occasions, on the other hand, efforts are made to attain some supposed spiritual gain by ignoring the rightful materialistic pursuits. In either case, the fine balance between the two is disturbed.

Under the bright sun-light of enhanced awareness, on the other hand, the entire gamut of human relationships gets illumined. As a result of such illumination, roles to be played by different individuals get clearly defined. Relationships are established more by choice rather than by instinct. Moreover, one becomes capable of realizing the limitations of privileges and importance of responsibilities of every role.

Such a situation leads to the establishment of solid foundations for smooth inter-personal relations, which in turn lead to a more satisfied individual and a more stable society.

Notes

Total and unconditional surrender before the Lord Leads to vitory over all one's weaknesses

Eight

Answers of Some Question An Attempt

Question: If the relationship between an individual and the Creator is an individual's personal affair, what role can organised religion play?

Answer: Historically speaking, religion had always been a constant source of strife. To a great extent, it continues to be so even today. It has also helped in the development of a parasitic class, which always tried to create hurdles in the path of unity of oneself with one's Creator. Such hurdles exist in every society in the form of rituals, dogmas and superstitions etc. Sometimes religious fanaticism attains such proportions that man, who is a creature of Nature, becomes subservient to an idea, which is of its own making and form becomes more important than the substance.

Religion draws artificial lines on the map of mankind. It creates exclusive and not-so-exclusive clubs where members are taught to treat the outsiders as less than equals. Not only that. Even natural calamities such as earthquakes are seen to be welcome if the majority of its victims belong to

the other community. Organized religion, which is generally based on the teachings of some one person, creates a god of its own choice, and expects everyone to believe in it. What matters, however, is the quality and intensity of one's faith in oneself and one's Creator and not the quality of the imagined god. Yet, it cannot be denied that the institution of religion has a great potential as a social and cultural force. If enlightened people use this tool wisely, it can play a very positive role in the social and cultural fields. However, it is clear that religion cannot make any big contribution in the spiritual attainment of an individual.

Question: What is good and what is bad? What is right and what is wrong? What is moral and what is immoral?

Answer: Nothing can be described as good or bad, right or wrong, moral or immoral in absolute terms. Any and every entity or object, be it organic or inorganic, represents, at a particular point of time, a form of Nature. Similarly, any and every action, resultant event and consequent changes of form, represent its dynamism. Then how can one be good and the other bad, one be right and the other wrong, or one be moral and the other immoral?

Speaking in relative terms, however, there are always two angles of looking at any object, action or event: individualistic and wholistic. Every organism, including of the human variety, has an innate right to judge objects, actions and events from its own perspective, and to accordingly label them as good or bad, moral or immoral, right or wrong. But this label keeps on varying from person to person, situation to situation, time to time. During individualistic judgment, another factor of uncertainty creeps in. One judges any action, thing or event from the point of view of one's perceived self-interest, without realising that what is perceived as self-interest by him at a particular point of time, may not actually be in his best interest at that point of time.

A wholistic view, comparatively speaking, is of a more durable nature. But even a wholistic view may be a restricted view in-as-much as it may be affected by considerations of race, class, state or religion etc. A view based on such considerations also changes, though not that frequently.

But the touchstone which can correctly label an action, event or object as moral or immoral, right or wrong, or good or bad, is whether that action, event or object conforms to the underlying principles of Nature or not. What are these principles? As discussed in this book in earlier chapters, they undoubtedly are happiness, peace, strength and kindness. These are essential ingredients of the self. Any action is right and moral if its intended, and not necessarily achieved, results are capable of enhancing any or all of the above mentioned conditions. A similar parameter has to be applied in judging the result of an action, which presents itself in the form of an event and / object.

Nature, over a period of billions of years, has evolved a complex network of various systems and sub-systems, which are not only interconnected and interdependent but also function in harmony with each other. Such harmony is essence of life and is also synonymous with other essential ingredients of self, that is happiness, peace etc.

Any action, which adversely affects the working of any system, and thereby the intra-system and inter-system harmony, cannot be described as right or moral. For the same reason, its results cannot be termed as good. For example, a system has been evolved by Nature to regenerate oxygen, which is essential for continuation of life on earth. Any action by an individual, group or humanity as a whole which creates hurdles in the proper functioning of this system cannot be termed as right and moral. Similarly, there is a system in place which, while allowing the sun's rays to reach the earth, protects life from their harmful effects. If some people dig holes in the ozone layer in search of momentary comfort, such actions are not only immoral but also suicidal for the entire existence.

In the same fashion, human body has evolved to transmit the truth. If an object or event is seen by the human eye, it is faithfully transmitted to the brain, which in turn relays it to the other organs. Suitable action follows. But if a message A is received by the brain, and the brain in turn is supposed to relay the message B, lots of extra steps have to be introduced. Upon receiving the message A, the brain consigns this message to the temporary memory chamber, and generates on its own message B. Then messages A and B are selectively relayed to different organs, and they are directed to act accordingly. For future references also, message A or message B becomes relevant as per the prevailing situation. In this process, lots of extra energy is consumed and lots of extra chemicals have to be produced by the body. This chemistry, in the long term, has adverse impact not only on the body but also on the mind-matter which is intimately connected to the body. Thus, telling a lie may have its own momentary benefits, but it carries a heavy cost in terms of physical and mental health. While in day-to-day life it may not always be possible to rely on truth and truth alone, but at the same time one must be aware of social, physiological and psychological costs which falsehood carries.

Thus, falsehood and its derivatives such as dishonesty, stealing etc. cannot be termed as right actions, because they do not work synergetically with the functioning of the human body.

In short, the only lasting and credible parameter that can be applied to judge any action, event or object, is whether or not it conforms to the scheme of things evolved by the Nature.

Question: Are the systems created by Nature unjust, as all individuals do not get equal opportunities for self-development? Some are born strong, some weak. Some are born rich, some poor. How can such a system be called just? How can such a system be called perfect?

Answer: Variety is the essence of life. Uniformity in all respects such as shape, size, colour etc. would render creation meaningless, as it would be nothing but repetition. Nature abhors repetition. If variety of creation is to have meaning, then every object, action and the resultant event, at any point of time, must represent a different shade of existence. As a consequence, each individual must not only be different from everyone else, but must also be placed in a different environment. As a natural corollary, some are stronger than the others, some are white while some are black, etc. In a nutshell, everyone is unique. Everyone has the distinction of being distinct.

Nature does not discriminate against anyone, including the nonhumans. It has only made everyone different.

Everyone perceives oneself to be inferior or superior, as compared to the others, as per the values acquired during one's existence. Based on individual perceptions, there comes into being a social perception. Some are perceived to be in a more advantageous or disadvantageous position than others in one or more respects. But are these comparisons and the resultant perceptions at all valid? Nature has created various entities, none of which is permanent. Everyone is changing every moment, everything is in a state of flux. Then how can one be compared with the other? Who is in competition with whom? Only those who take life on 'as-is-where-is' basis can enjoy it thoroughly. But it must be appreciated, at the same time, that to be in sync with the universe which is so dynamic, one has to adopt a policy which is pro-active rather than re-active.

Moreover, sometimes, a perceived disadvantage engulfs the whole of one's being. A part overshadows the whole. In this regard, it must not be forgotten that any perceived disadvantage, howsoever real, is only a very small part of life. What is required is that one should exploit one's comparative advantages to the maximum extent possible.

It must be reiterated that nature is unjust to none. Everyone has one's own strengths and weaknesses. The art of living lies in building on one's strengths and overcoming one's weaknesses.

This issue of disparate positioning can be examined in a slightly different perspective also. Any situation in which one finds oneself can be broadly categorised as a *comfort situation* or a *challenge situation*. In a comfort situation, one gets what one wants without much effort. In a challenge situation, on the other hand, one may not be able to achieve the desired results even after sincere hard work. Since the comfort situation satisfies one's desires easily, it is perceived to be good and, hence, just. The challenge situation, on the other hand, is perceived to be unjust, for it makes us work at achieving our targets or goals.

Comfort situation, though perceived to be good and just, carries its own hidden cost. In such a situation, theoretically speaking, one is likely to get all the comforts of life without much hard work, that is, without a proportionate use of mind and body. Faculties that are not used regularly start loosing their sheen. A person who is not used to walking in day-to-day life may not be in a position to save himself if required to run for life. Similarly, mental faculties also become subdued if not used regularly. Luxurious life, in fact, is a dull life. It is only in a life full of challenges, which is otherwise considered as unjust, that one gets an opportunity to prove one's worth. One gets stronger mentally and physically. In a challenge situation, one's real self comes to the fore and an individual evolves further. Therefore, it cannot be said as to which of the two situations is in the best interest of the individual: the comfort situation or the challenge situation.

Moreover, no situation can be described as pure comfort situation or a pure challenge situation. Life is a continuous but varying blend of the two. Thus, it is very difficult to describe any situation as better or worse, just or unjust. It is only human perception that makes it to look like one or the other. The conclusion remains the same, namely that Nature is unjust to none.

Nature can never be called imperfect, either. It has very definite and precise laws of governance, which are applicable to everyone, irrespective of his race, caste, colour or creed. It is only due to a lack of understanding that Nature gives an impression of being imperfect.

Question: How does substance compare with form, consciousness with mind and body?

Answer: There can be no form without substance, for vacuum, by its very definition, cannot have any form. Substance without form, on the other hand, has no means to express itself. Thus, for life to be maintained, both are equally important. Which of the two is more real? If substance is the perennial reality, form is the reality of the moment. For any particular moment, one is as real as the other. To ignore one would be as fatal as to ignore the other. Substance, in one form or the other, was always there and would always be. Thus, substance is permanent and form is permanently in flux.

Question: What role do the legacies of experiences play in the day-to-day life of a person?

Answer: Behavioral pattern of a person is determined more by the contents of his sub-conscious mind than the situations in which he is placed from time to time. One finds oneself placed in different situations at different times. Legacies appropriate to the given situation come to the surface and play their role in determining the

behaviour of the concerned person. For example, in a situation where one's desires get frustrated, legacies of anger rush up and, unless controlled with a strong will power, one gets angry. Since this anger occurs in a particular situation, it is attributed by the individual to the situation rather than to his own mental make up. With an understanding of the true nature of legacies as well as a strong will-power, both of which can be attained by an enhanced awareness, one's behaviour can to a great extent be insulated from the outside situations.

Question: What role does awareness play in day-to-day life?

Answer: Enhanced awareness, in fact, can change the whole perspective of one's life. To illustrate, when one gets aware of one's breathing, one can realise that he is not making full use of a substantial part of that wonderful machine that nature has provided to him, that is the lungs. Thus aware breathing is bound to be deep breathing, which can bring about a revolutionary change in one's physical and mental make-up. Similarly, all mental tension gets dissipated under the influence of enhanced awareness, because the source of all tensions, that is legacies of experiences, gets exposed when one is in a state of enhanced awareness. Intense but equanimous observation can be described as a key to enhanced awareness. Also, under the influence of enhanced awareness, when one understands the difference between micro and macro level egos, one's perspective of looking at oneself and the world as a whole widens, and one ceases to be petty-minded.

There is no end to the road to awareness, only a beginning. Anyone can start walking on it at any time; but the first step taken on this road is the most important step.

It must, however, be understood that enhanced awareness may not eliminate all hurdles of life, but it certainly would equip one to face them boldly.

Question: What is the importance of time in one's life?

Answer: Any feelings or sentiments experienced by mind-matter at any point in time can, under no circumstances, be altered at another point of time. Today's joy howsoever intense cannot erase the memory of yesterday's sorrow, because no two events, and consequently by the accompanying feelings, separated in time even by a small fraction of a second, can overlap each other. The scar remains forever i.e. till the mind-body complex survives. Thus, those who live in the memories of the past or the dreams of the future, live in a fool's paradise. Live in the present, an aware present, at the place you are situated.

Question: What is the role of one's mistakes in life?

Answer: One learns from others' mistakes also. But it is one's own follies from which one learns the most. Don't hide them. Don't be ashamed of them. Learn to respect them for what they are - a great teacher.

Question: What is the role of machines in human life?

Answer: Mind-body complex is a perfect machine in itself, which is capable of performing mainly the following four functions:

1. Motor functions i.e. physical work done by the body;
2. Computing i.e. work done by the brain;
3. Feelings i.e. sentiments, which fall in the domain of mind; and
4. Awareness i.e. the function of being aware.

Many aspects of the first two functions have already been taken over by machines. Efforts are now on to develop machines, which can take over some aspects of functions of the third category also.

In the process of evolution, a part of body which is not used for long becomes dysfunctional. Warning bells in this regard have already started ringing. It is feared that boredom is going to be the 'silent killer of the future' as brain and other organs of the body will have less and less work to perform. Thank god, no machine has so far been visualised which can be aware of itself.

Question: Is there life after death?

Answer: How does it matter? What is more important is how one lives life and what one achieves in life. Anyhow, one thing is sure. Individual entities, be they organic or inorganic, come into being and fade away from time to time, but awareness always remains, either in its manifested or the *un-manifested* form.

There is another way of looking at it. One of the most important ingredients of life is the capability to consciously participate in the perennial chain of events. Participation leads to influencing. This capability to influence does not necessarily vanish with the physical fading away of an entity. Thus, an individual can continue to influence the affairs of the world, much after he ceases to exist in the

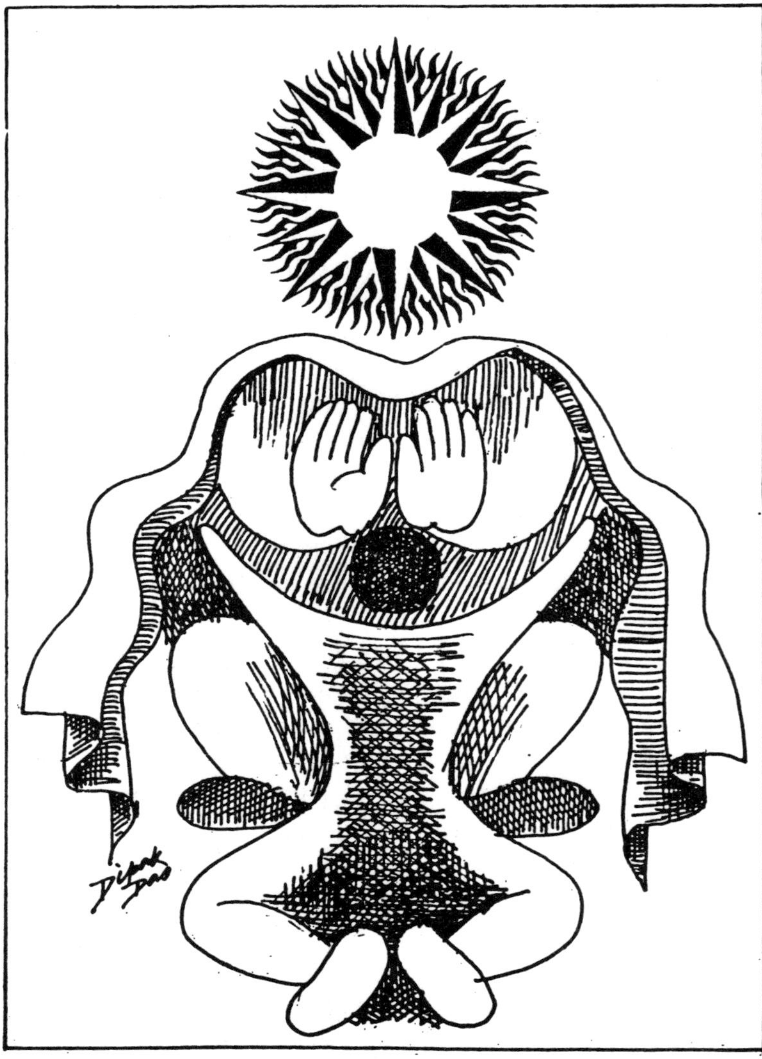

physical form. He continues to participate in the chain of events, albeit in an indirect manner. A Buddha, a Christ, a Shankar, a Nanak or a Newton has greater influence on our life today than many of the living beings. In that sense of the term, they are alive long after their physical demise.

In fact, death is only a form of life as it has its own influence on the chain of events.

Question: How important is the role of a teacher in the realisation of Truth?

Answer: Broadly speaking, knowledge can be divided into three categories, namely, knowledge relating to areas covered by physical sciences such as physics, chemistry, biology etc., knowledge of social sciences such as philosophy, sociology, political science etc., and knowledge of the self. Out of the three, only knowledge of the self has the potential of leading one to realise the Truth.

It is almost impossible to achieve thorough, or even functional knowledge of physical sciences without the able guidance of a good teacher. However, as regards the knowledge of social sciences, role of the teacher may not be that crucial.

As far as acquiring knowledge of the self is concerned, what is most crucial is an enhanced awareness, because awareness is the medium through which one can understand oneself. It is the individual concerned who has to slowly and steadily move on the path of awareness and eventual realisation of the Truth. However, a teacher has a vital role to play in such a realisation. He has not only to show the right path but also to ensure that there are no major deviations. To put it differently, everyone has to search for the Truth himself. A wise man, however, can help by providing a road map and pointing towards the pitfalls. Here, a word of caution. Sometimes the teacher is made out to be as important as the object of realisation itself, which is not correct. Thus, the teacher has an important role to play in the realisation of Truth, but the two cannot be placed on the same pedestal.

Question: If Nature is not omnipotent and is partial to none, then why pray and why surrender oneself to it?

Answer: When *unmanifested*, Nature is pure consciousness without any form. It is unchanging and unchangeable. In its manifested form also, its basic characteristics remain the same, that is, an unchanging Reality with an ever changing face.

God is certainly not someone sitting on a throne in Heaven and dispensing justice through a network of trusted courtiers and other complimentary staff. Nor does He need to send messengers to the earth from time to time to spread some supposed truth. Mankind, in fact, has been provided by Nature with enough intelligence and awareness to find out the truth on its own, at least in bits and pieces, through experience.

Nature is as much bound by its own laws as anyone else. It cannot play favouritism games on the basis of race, religion or some such other consideration. Favours cannot be granted on the basis of how much one remembers some supposedly supernatural power. For Nature, everyone is equally important as everyone is an integral and inalienable part of Itself.

What makes appreciable difference in one's life, however, is how one visualises God and what sort of relationship one establishes with Him. Imagine a statue lying in the centre of a circle and different people sitting on its periphery trying to draw its image. No two drawings can tally with each other even though the statue remains the same. Everyone views the statue from its own angle. Similarly, everyone visualises Reality in his/her own way and establishes a unique relationship with it. This relationship influences one's personality in a big way.

When one prays sincerely to the Lord without any, or even for, some materialistic gains and surrenders himself completely before Him, one may not get immediate materialistic rewards, but. one does come very close to the Reality and establish a very close contact with Him. Under the influence of such a contact, one's false ego melts down, and the walls of ignorance start crumbling. One realises oneself to be nothing but happiness, strength, peace and kindness. That is how, by surrendering oneself before the Lord, one can attain complete peace of mind, which is otherwise so elusive.

In the ultimate analysis, for an individual, what matters most is not the Reality as it exists, but what he perceives it to be, and the sort of relationship he establishes with it.

Even more important than the nature of relationship is the intensity of that relationship. The heat of intensified relationship causes all doubt to evaporate and, in the process, helps one to clearly see the reality as it exists, and one's own role in such existence. Thus, in order to lead a happy and successful life, what is important is to acquire knowledge about the Truth, establish an appropriate relationship with it, and maintain the intensity of that relationship.

Question: Why are some people concerned more about recognition and appreciation of their perceived achievements by others, rather than the achievements themselves?

Answer: As discussed in earlier chapters, one generates an image of oneself in the mirror of consciousness, an ego. This image does not necessarily match with the objective reality which is often reflected through the eyes of other persons. There is always a gap between the two. This difference between self-image and objective reality creates a persistent sense of dissatisfaction in the mind of the concerned individual. More the difference, more the dissatisfaction. This sense of dissatisfaction erodes one's confidence in oneself.

To overcome the feelings of constant dissatisfaction, one tries to narrow down the gap between self-image and the reality by seeking approval and appreciation from others. Relief provided by such techniques is only temporary. In fact, an appreciation, if false, can widen this gap in the long run by further inflating one's self-image.

Since the chasm between one's self-image and the reality is created by one's own perception, it can be filled up, or at least narrowed down, by the concerned individual only. First step in that direction is taken the moment one realises the existence of such a gap and the need to narrow it down. Only after such a realisation can one inquire into the source of this gap and try to find ways and means to eliminate it. Such a situation leads one to understand that persistent sense of dissatisfaction cannot be overcome by seeking approval and appreciation from others, especially because they themselves can be biased in favour of or against the concerned person. Moreover, they themselves may not be enlightened enough to approve or disapprove the action of the concerned individual. Even self-praise does not help in controlling the sense of dissatisfaction for long. Long lasting satisfaction can only be achieved by basing one's self-image on objective reality so that it is as near to the reality as possible. In such a situation, the gap between reality and its perception is minimized to the extent possible, and the persistent sense of dissatisfaction which arises as a result of such a gap automatically comes under control.

Correct imaging of oneself imparts tremendous confidence to oneself whereby one can achieve success after success without being concerned about the approval or disapproval of others.

Question: What is the role of fate in one's life?

Answer: Fate is nothing but a peg on which one can conveniently hang one's failures. In many situations, when one becomes helpless, the concept of fate can act as a good shock absorber. To that extent, it plays a useful role. However, it should never be allowed to become an excuse for non-performance.

Question: Can the future be predicted?

Answer: No one knows for certain as to whether the future can be predicted or not. But one thing is sure. It can certainly be influenced and it can certainly be manipulated. If the present could be represented as the *xth* link in the perennial chain of events, then the future would be represented as $x+1$, $x+2$ .... $x+n$. The common ingredient in all these links is x. If x is managed properly, then $x+n$ is automatically taken care of. Thus, it follows that future can certainly be improved by improving the present.

Question: How can stress be managed?

Answer: What is stress? In common parlance, stress can be described as a state of mind which is characterised by fear and apprehension without an apparent cause. As discussed in earlier chapters, it arises due to wrong interpretation of one's role in the perennial chain of events and also due to ignorance about the nature of the web of relationships into which one is seemingly entrapped.

Stress need not be managed or controlled. It manages itself, once the nature of stress and the source of its origin become clear.

Enhanced awareness is the perfect antidote to stressful conditions. When one becomes aware of one's own thought process, one realises that the stress condition is neither due to the load of work nor to the other external factors. One realises that stress is an internal condition. Instead of blaming others for one's miseries, one starts analysing one's own weaknesses and accordingly starts taking corrective steps. In such circumstances stress and strain vanish almost completely.

Question: What is the most effective manner in which one can lead a contented, successful and purposeful life?

Answer: First of all, what is essential for anyone to succeed is to identify one's aim in life, for an aimless life is a useless life. Here, a word of caution. Road to success is neither uni-dimensional nor straight. It is not unidimensional in-as-much as succees in any one of the three spheres of life, that is, materialistic, intellectual or spiritual, may although bring name and fame to the concerned person, yet it cannot be called wholistic success. Since gross and fine matter, and also physical and thought energy are only forms of superfine matter and consciousness energy respectively, it may not be difficult to achieve reasonable success in all the three aspects of life simultaneously. Further, the metaphorical road to success often passes through ditches of failures. Thus, one has to identify different goals at different times. Then action has to be planned and executed to achieve these goals. But a successful life does not in any way guarantee a contented life.

To develop a synergy between success, contentment and purposefulness, the best way is to surrender oneself completely before God. When one does so, ego almost merges with the self, and as a result there is no ego other than the self, that is awareness. Thus, there is no one to claim the authorship of actions and, therefore, of their results. Nor does anyone own the successes or disown the failures. In such a situation, one goes through the experiences of life without generating any legacies. As such, there is no fear. There is no feeling of guilt. There is no tension. Moreover, as the decisions are guided more by logic and reason and less by irrational thought, there is a greater chance of success. In such circumstances, one can lead a successful and purposeful life free from all worries. In short, when one surrenders oneself completely before the Lord, one gains almost complete control over oneself.

One is happy not because of what one has, but because of what one is.

Be aware, habitually